Developing Literacy
NON-FICTION

READING AND WRITING
ACTIVITIES FOR THE LITERACY HOUR

year

Christine Moorcroft

Series consultant: Ray Barker

A & C BLACK

Contents

Writing composition

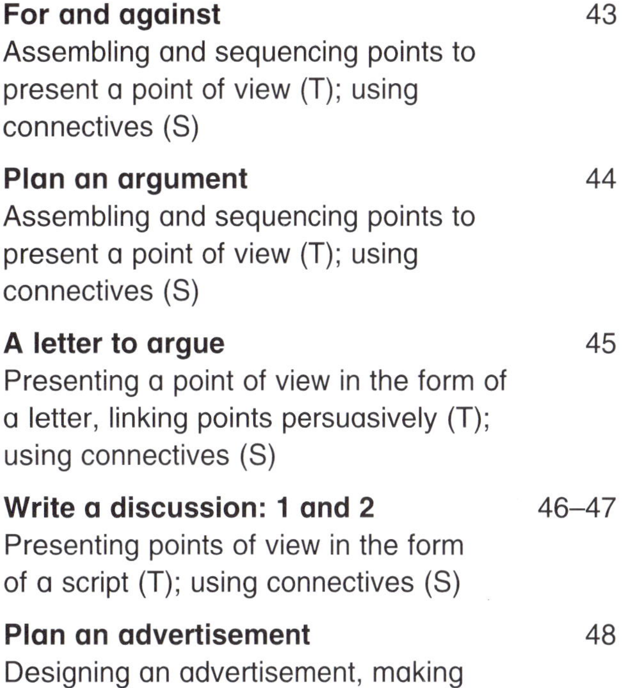

Acknowledgements
The author and publishers are grateful for permission to reproduce the following:
p. 22 text adapted from a leaflet by The Wildlife Trust, 80 York Way, London N1 9NG.
The publishers apologise for the few instances in which they have been unable to make contact with the copyright holders, and would be grateful if they would contact the publishers.

Published 2002 by
A & C Black (Publishers) Limited
37 Soho Square, London W1D 3QZ

ISBN 0-7136-6068-6

Copyright text © Christine Moorcroft, 2002
Copyright illustrations © Liz McIntosh, 2002
Copyright cover illustration © Alison Dexter, 2002

The author and publishers would like to thank Ray Barker, Madeleine Madden, Julia Tappin and Sarah Vickers for their advice in producing this series of books.

A CIP catalogue record for this book is available from the British Library.

Printed in Great Britain by The Cromwell Press Ltd, Trowbridge, Wiltshire.

Developing Literacy: Non-fiction is a series of seven photocopiable activity books for the Literacy Hour. Each book provides a range of non-fiction reading and writing activities, and supports the teaching of reading and writing skills at text, sentence and word levels.

The activities are designed to be carried out in the time allocated to independent work during the Literacy Hour. They incorporate strategies which encourage independent learning: for example, ways in which children can evaluate their own work or that of a partner.

The reading activities develop the children's study and research skills (reading for a purpose, understanding and interpreting, and making use of what they have read) and provide models on which they can base their own writing.

The writing activities concentrate on the purpose of a text, the audience for whom it is written and the context in which it is to be read, and encourage the children to be aware of these considerations when they write.

The activities in **Year 4** reinforce word, text and sentence-level skills and encourage the children to:

- develop an awareness of the purposes of opening sentences;

- pick out the key phrases and sentences which convey information and opinions;

- develop an awareness of the ways in which electronic texts are designed to be read;

- develop skills in quickly preparing for research by reviewing what they already know, what they need to find out, the available sources of information (and appraising them to check which are the most useful) and presenting their notes from different sources in an organised format;

- scan a printed or electronic text to find out what it is about, skim it to find useful headings, phrases or sentences and use these as tools for summarising it;

- monitor their own understanding of a text and develop strategies to make sense of difficult texts;

- develop skills in marking extracts in a way which helps them to make notes;

- write notes quickly and efficiently in a way which is suitable for their purpose and fill out these notes to produce connected prose;

- understand how paragraphs are used in organising and sequencing information;

- develop an awareness of the significant features and conventions of different types of non-fiction text and how they are suited to the purpose of the text (instructions, explanatory texts, arguments, discussions, non-chronological reports, newspaper reports and persuasive texts, including advertisements), and to use the features and conventions in their own writing;

- write summaries of sentences, paragraphs and chapters.

The National Literacy Strategy and non-fiction

The National Literacy Strategy *Framework for Teaching* encourages teachers to use all kinds of non-fiction texts, both printed and electronic: for example, reports and articles from newspapers and magazines giving facts, information, explanations and opinions; information books and CD-ROMs giving facts and explanations; advertisements from different media; leaflets and flyers; and discussion texts such as editorials and reviews.

Links to other subjects

The children can use their literacy skills to further their learning in other subjects, through the reading of shared texts or guided reading during the Literacy Hour and by using and developing their research skills at other times. During the Literacy Hour, the children can write about what they have learned in other subjects and learn how to select the best methods for their writing.

Using non-fiction in the Literacy Hour

While the activities in this book focus on the independent part of the Literacy Hour, the notes on pages 6 to 8 and at the foot of each activity page suggest a variety of ways you can introduce non-fiction reading and writing, present whole-class activities and use the plenary session to conclude the lesson. The ideas support the following strategies:

- **demonstrating** or modelling the way in which an experienced reader and writer tackles a skill or approach to reading or writing, by 'thinking aloud' about what you are doing;

- **sharing** an activity: the teacher or other adult (as the expert) takes responsibility for the difficult parts of the activity, while the learners take responsibility for the easier parts. The learners then gradually take over some of the more difficult parts. This bridges the gap between demonstration and independent work;

- **supporting** an activity, in which the children undertake the activity independently, with the teacher (or other adult) monitoring and being ready to offer support when necessary. This avoids the difficulties which arise when the teacher moves from demonstration or modelling to asking the children to work independently.

Children will benefit from learning the following strategies to help them read and write non-fiction:

- **predicting** (suggesting what information a book or page might provide, and how they can tell);

- **clarifying** (working out ways in which to understand new or difficult words and ideas);

- **questioning** (saying what questions the text raises and what it makes them want to find out);

- **summarising** (saying in a limited number of words what the text is about and what it tells them).

The activities in this book support the following stages of the children's interactions with text:

- **bringing to mind what they already know** about the subject (for example, by making flow-charts, diagrams and lists);

- **deciding what they want to find out** (for example, writing questions);

- **deciding where to find the information they need** (for example, information books, electronic texts, people and websites);

- **learning the best ways in which to use the source** (from the teacher or other adult, who models the use of the source);

- **developing strategies to help them understand the text** (for example, marking difficult words or passages, and re-phrasing or transferring information from prose to charts or from diagrams to prose);

- **recording information** (using charts and note-making strategies such as abbreviation);

- **evaluating the information** (for example, evaluating the validity of the source or comparing information from different sources, and separating facts from opinions);

- **communicating information** (considering the audience, purpose and context of the text to be written and their effects on language and layout).

Extension activities

Most of the activity sheets end with a challenge (**Now try this!**) which reinforces and extends the children's learning and provides the teacher with an opportunity for assessment. These more challenging activities might be appropriate for only a few children; it is not expected that the whole class should complete them.

On some pages there is space for the children to complete the extension activities, but for others they will need a notebook or a separate sheet of paper.

Organisation

The activities require very few resources besides scissors, glue, word-banks and a range of dictionaries. Other materials are specified in the teachers' notes on the activity pages.

The notes below expand upon those which are provided at the foot of each activity page. They give ideas and suggestions for making the most of the activity sheet, including suggestions for the whole-class introduction, the plenary session or for follow-up work using an adapted version of the activity sheet. To help teachers select appropriate learning experiences for their pupils, the activities are grouped into sections, but the pages need not be presented in the order in which they appear in the book, unless otherwise stated.

Reading comprehension

The activities in this section reinforce the children's word-level and sentence-level skills and develop their ability to read, use and understand the structure and language style of newspaper and magazine reports, instructions, non-chronological reports, information books, explanatory, discursive and promotional texts (including advertisements), editorials and various electronic texts. The activities encourage children to plan their work by bringing to mind what they already know, formulating questions and then locating the answers in non-fiction texts. They help the children to distinguish between information and opinion and to use the features of different types of non-fiction texts to find information. The children learn how to appraise a non-fiction book to decide how well it will provide relevant information, to scan the book to find that information and to skim-read before deciding which parts to annotate and make notes from. They develop skills in summarising texts and organising notes from different sources.

Which type of text? (page 9). This activity develops the children's ability to identify the features of different types of non-fiction texts. Once they have identified each type of text they could describe its audience and purpose and consider the context in which it might be used. You could discuss the ways in which the audience, purpose and context affect the language, style and structure of the text: for example, a note to oneself is written in an informal style (perhaps in note form or a form of shorthand only understood by the writer); a dictionary and telephone directory are arranged in alphabetical order to help the user find an entry quickly.

Quiz quest (page 10). This activity helps the children to use information texts efficiently. Suggest that they say what they are doing step by step, and model how to do this: 'Check the contents, look for key words in the index, make a note of the page numbers, skim the pages,' or 'Check the opening page, look for 'hot spots', click on them and skim the pages.' Different groups of children could use different sources to answer the same question, and note which was the most efficient.

Answers: Nepal (use an atlas); the furcula or wishbone (use a dictionary); beagle (use information books about dogs, combined with pictures from Snoopy comics, also the Snoopy website: www.snoopy.com); answers will vary (use a calendar or diary); answers will vary (use a local businesses and services directory or telephone directory).

Capturing interest (page 11). This draws attention to the ways in which writers use the opening sentence of a non-fiction text to capture the interest of readers and to set the scene and tone of the text.

Look for the facts (page 12). This activity encourages the children to skim-read a text to find information. They could identify any phrases and sentences which engage the readers' interest and make them want to read on.

Fact or opinion? (page 13). This activity develops the children's ability to distinguish between fact and opinion. This could be introduced by reading out statements and asking the children to hold up a card on which is written 'F' (fact) or 'O' (opinion); those who hold up the wrong card are 'out', while one of the others has to explain why he or she is right. Ask the children where they can check each fact.

What's the story? 1 and 2 (pages 14–15). These pages focus on the ways in which a headline and sub-heading can be used not only to give information about a newspaper story but also to set the tone of the article.

Read all about it! (page 16). This activity develops the children's skills in identifying the key features of newspaper articles. Encourage them to discuss how each feature helps the reader. The children could analyse other newspaper articles in the same way. **Write all about it!** (page 33) provides a structure to help them write their own newspaper-style reports.

Formal or informal? (page 17). Here the children are encouraged to notice the differences in style between formal and informal newspaper articles. They could analyse other newspaper articles in the same way and note which newspapers tend to be formal or informal. It will be useful first to give the children some practice in changing verbs from the active to passive voice (see *Developing Literacy: Sentence Level*).

Instructions test (page 18). This activity focuses on the general features of instructional texts and the features and conventions which are specific to particular types of instructions. Encourage the children to consider how they help the reader (for example, it is essential to provide a picture of a model to be made and it is helpful to give a photograph of a cake to be prepared in a recipe, but not necessary for a soup).

Electronic text review (page 19). This activity focuses on the features of electronic texts which help the reader to locate information. The children could compare the ways in which they use features of electronic and printed texts: for example an electronic text, like a printed text, might have a contents (or 'opening') page and an index, but the contents might be scrolled and the index might be used by clicking on a letter and then scrolling down for a key word; the opening page of an electronic text might also be used by clicking on 'hot spots' which take the user directly to the required information.

Ready for research and **Will it help?** (pages 20 and 21). These pages provide structures to support the children in preparing for factual research. Children could compare their choice of 'most useful sources' (page 20) with that of a partner who is researching the same question. Point out the importance of recording what can be found out from each page or chapter they have noted so that they can return to it to find the exact information they want.

Is it clear? (page 22). This encourages the children to think about what they are reading by annotating and marking extracts from a text, checking that they understand it, developing strategies for monitoring their own understanding and taking action when they come across something they do not understand (rather than skimming over and ignoring it).

Summary match (page 23). This activity focuses on the use of paragraphs to structure a recount chronologically. It also provides a model of how to summarise each paragraph in preparation for **An explanation** (page 24), which is structured logically rather than chronologically. This leads on to **Features of explanations** (page 25), which develops the children's understanding of the structure and language of explanations.

Arguments: 1 and **2**, **Structure an argument** and **A discussion** (pages 26–29). These activities encourage the children to consider the structure and features of arguments and discussions. The children could look for other features of arguments not included in the activities (for example, the tense used) and they might notice the use of expressions which begin 'it would', 'there should' and 'if'. This will prepare for later work on subjunctives and conditionals. The children could contribute to a class word-bank of useful connectives to use in arguments.

Persuasion and **Come and buy!** (pages 30 and 31). These pages show that some texts present information in a way which persuades people to buy something, do something or go somewhere. Explain that information can be expressed so that it does more than just present facts. The children first need to have read and listened to different types of advertisements and noticed the impressions they create and the ways in which the advertisers do this. They could write a factual report about a place they know and then change the report, adding persuasive adjectives. They could also use copies of the chart on page 31 to analyse other advertisements. Ask them to consider other features: for example, the layout of advertisements (including the use of colour, bullet points and flashes and why some parts are in large print and others in small print). **Plan an advertisement** (page 48) provides a structure and hints to help the children write in the style of advertisements.

Target practice (page 32). This develops the children's skills in summarising. Possible answers to discuss include: 'Most of the class want a shorter afternoon break and an earlier finish,' 'The villagers held a race,' 'The old woman in the shoe had ten daughters and seven sons,' 'Wind, rain and low temperatures were forecast,' and 'Costumes at the fancy dress party included animals, clowns and fairies.'

Writing comprehension

These activities develop the children's skills in making notes in a way which supports their writing for different purposes. There are structures which enable the children to organise their writing for different audiences, purposes and contexts and to use appropriate styles of language: for example, writing in the style of newspaper articles and writing instructions, non-chronological reports, explanations, arguments, reports and advertisements.

Write all about it! (page 33). This helps the children to use the structure and key features of a newspaper report in their own writing. It encourages them to make notes and re-draft their work. **Read all about it!** (page 16) can be used as an example of the style of newspaper reports.

Make it fit: 1 and 2 (pages 34–35). These pages develop the children's skills in writing briefly. You could ask the children first to identify the main points of the story and then to find and cross out any complete sentences which are not necessary.

Writing instructions (page 36). This provides the children with a structure to help them write instructions, especially with regard to the order of the steps. The children should write in note form in the boxes. Encourage them to read and try to follow each other's instructions in order to evaluate them.

Keep it short (page 37). This activity reinforces the children's ability to recognise and record key words and phrases from their reading (see also pages 11 and 12, which focus on reading rather than writing). It helps the children to understand that, when making notes, some of the words they read are more important than others.

Different sources: 1 and 2 (pages 38–39). These pages provide notes about the same topic (from different sources) and a structure to help the children organise the notes under sub-headings, which can be used as the basis for paragraphs in a report.

From notes to sentences (page 40). This activity gives examples of the ways in which words can be shortened or omitted when making notes. It provides a strategy for writing a report based on those notes.

Notes on a diagram (page 41). This activity encourages the children to organise their notes under headings which provide a paragraphing structure for their writing. The children could write an information passage based on their notes but without looking back at the original. Using this process encourages the children to think about what they read and to write in their own words rather than copying out sentences from books.

How does it work? (page 42). This activity helps the children to use the conventions of explanation writing: use of the present tense, the third person and a procedural structure.

For and against and **Plan an argument** (pages 43 and 44). These pages develop the children's skills in organising notes for a purpose. They present arguments in the form of statements (or assertions) supported by evidence and linked by logical connectives, and include the paragraphing of an argument. See also **Arguments: 1 and 2** (pages 26–27).

A letter to argue (page 45). This activity revises the conventions of formal letter-writing and provides a structure and hints which help the children to organise an argument in the form of a letter. To enable them to concentrate on the structure and organisation of the argument without having to research the content, they could re-write arguments which appear earlier in the book (see pages 26–28). Alternatively, the children could research a topic before beginning the activity sheet.

Write a discussion: 1 and 2 (pages 46–47). These pages help the children to distinguish between assertions and reasons or evidence in a discussion. The format of these pages takes the children through the process of constructing a discussion. Before beginning the activity, the children could listen to a television or radio discussion and notice how the contributors support their opinions with facts. Note that such discussions are not scripted. The children's scripts could be written as though they were the records of discussions which have taken place.

Plan an advertisement (page 48). This activity encourages the children to think about the effects of advertisements and how they are achieved (see **Come and buy!**, page 31). It provides ideas to help them think of lists of words which they could use in an advertisement and encourages them to consider the effects of these words. They could first brainstorm the impressions which advertisements for different products might want to create (for example, healthy, wholesome, reliable, exciting, sophisticated and so on), and discuss how to achieve them.

Which type of text?

Which type of text is each example?

- **Write in the boxes.**

1. Check that the seal is not broken.
2. Wash and dry the cut or graze.
3. Choose a plaster of the right size for

There are more than a hundred stalls in the market. The main things sold there are clothes, but there are many

Polish shoes, feed Tibs, empty bin, take Skipper for a walk

Case, A.	2 Old St	373 5012
Case, B.	1 Top St	374 0366
Case, W.	31 Key Lane	287 1191

S

silent (adj.) Without any sound.
since (prep.) From (a

The first thing we heard was a bang and then an engine starting. Next we saw two men running round the corner. Before long we

- **Explain your answers.**

- **Make a chart for different types of non-fiction texts.**

Title	Type of text	What I noticed about the language

Teachers' note Before the children begin the activity, show them examples of different types of non-fiction texts and talk about their content, layout, structure, language and style (including the kind of subject-matter; the use of layout features such as headings and sub-headings, colour and bold text; how formal the language is; the person, tense and form of the verb, and so on).

Developing Literacy
Non-fiction Year 4
© A & C Black 2002

Quiz quest

- **Find the answer as quickly as you can.**

Question	Answer	Text used		Write what you did, step by step, to find the answer
		Book, CD-ROM or Internet?	Title or website address	
In which country is Kathmandu?				
In birds such as turkeys, what is a merrythought?				
What breed of dog is Snoopy?				
On which day of the week is Christmas Day this year?				
What is the telephone number of your local library?				

- **Use a different text to check one of your answers.**
- **Write about which text was easier to use.**

Teachers' note The children need access to a range of different types of printed and electronic information texts. Model how to find the answer to a question by scanning the contents and index of a printed text or CD-ROM reference text, or the opening page of a website, and then by skim-reading the appropriate pages.

**Developing Literacy
Non-fiction Year 4
© A & C Black 2002**

Capturing interest

The opening words of a text can set the scene, set the tone and capture the reader's interest.

- **Match the** openings **to the texts.**
- **Write down why each opening is suitable.**

Openings

Dusk was spreading over the forest floor. Then suddenly, silent as a ghost, something large and dark stepped into a space among the trees about ten metres ahead.

The owners insist they were simply trying to knock down the fireplace.

Take a trip to Warwick Castle and explore 1000 years of history.

You'd be lucky to spot an octopus.

Nothing compares with the thrill of seeing tiny shoots come from a seed or a little shoot develop fat, healthy roots.

This creamy cheese dressing is perfect with a salad of fresh herbs mixed with green leaves and crispy bacon.

Texts

A leaflet about a historical site	A recipe
A newspaper report about an old farmhouse which fell down just before it was to be made a listed building. Its owners wanted to sell the land to a builder.	A chapter from an information book about the ways in which animals hide or disguise themselves
A story of an explorer's quest to find the yeti	The script from a television programme on gardening

Teachers' note You could introduce the activity by discussing one of the openings together. Ask the children what it tells them about the text: they should say what type of text it is and how they can tell, and predict what the text will be about. Features to point out include person, form of verbs (for example, questioning or commanding) and tense.

Developing Literacy
Non-fiction Year 4
© A & C Black 2002

Look for the facts

This text comes from a leaflet. Its purpose is to make people want to visit the place. It also gives information.

- **Underline the key words which give information.**

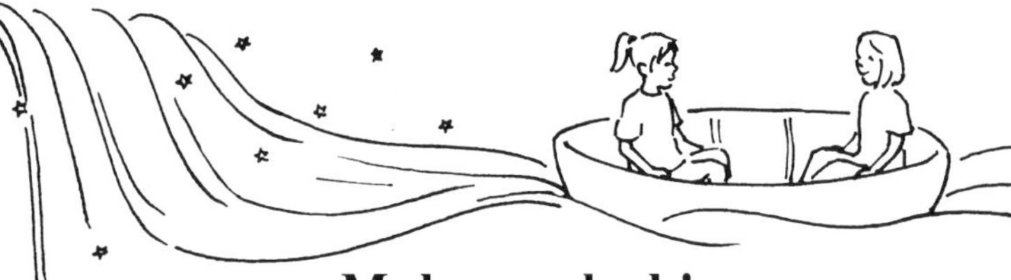

Make a splash!

Come to the all-weather sun and water centre where the sun always shines and there is never a drop of rain from January to December.

It's always summer in this <u>indoor</u> water-fun venue with the outdoor feel. With an air temperature kept at 22°C, you're never cold.

Slither down the Snake Slide into the foaming froth. The Snake Slide is 200 metres long, curving and curling its way round the Magic Mountain into a one-metre-deep pool with its super frothing jets. It is supervised at all times: 'Safe Fun' is our motto.

Play in the Fairy Fountain with its coloured jets of water to surprise you from all directions. Try to guess where the next one will come from!

If you want to stay dry while you enjoy the water, take a trip in a Cool Coracle from the Magic Spring, along the gently flowing Romantic River, through beautiful gardens which are in bloom all the year round.

- **List the** `facts` **you can find in the leaflet.**

1. The venue is indoors.

- **List words and phrases that make the centre seem interesting or exciting.**

Teachers' note You could begin by discussing the purpose of information texts. Point out the importance of capturing the reader's attention with an interesting or eye-catching opening, and maintaining it through a lively style. The children could collect examples of 'interesting' and 'boring' information texts and explain how they formed their opinions.

**Developing Literacy
Non-fiction Year 4
© A & C Black 2002**

Fact or opinion?

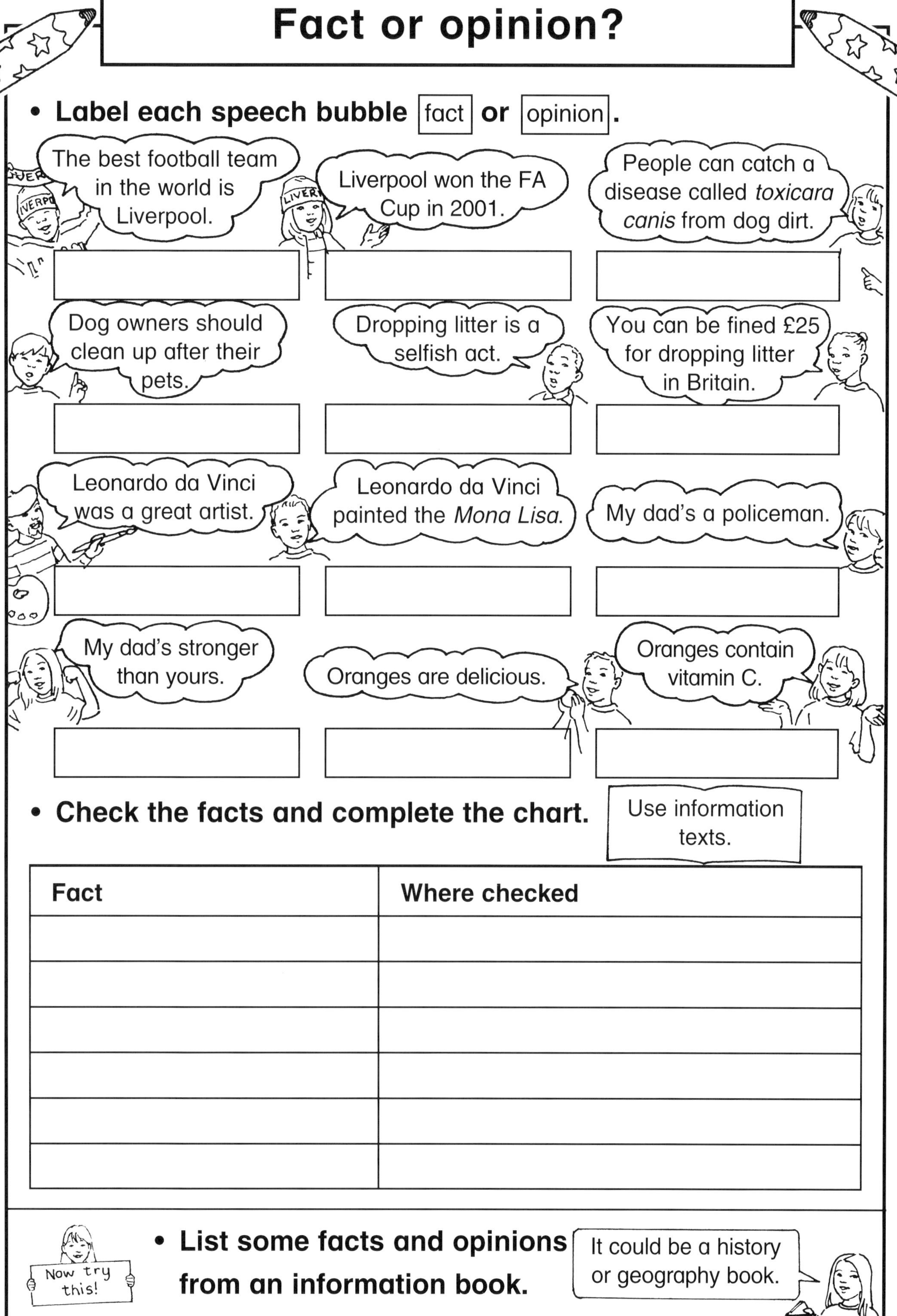

• **Label each speech bubble** fact **or** opinion .

• **Check the facts and complete the chart.**

Use information texts.

Fact	Where checked

• **List some facts and opinions from an information book.**

Now try this!

It could be a history or geography book.

Teachers' note It is useful to begin by revising the meaning of 'fact' (a statement which can be checked or proved) and 'opinion' (what someone thinks about a thing or idea). You could point out that sometimes opinions are expressed as though they were facts: for example, 'This is the tidiest classroom in the school.'

Developing Literacy
Non-fiction Year 4
© A & C Black 2002

What's the story? 1

- **Predict what these newspaper stories might be about.**
- **Write notes on the chart about the main points.**

	The people	What they did	Where (if known)
BEACH BRAWL SHAME Two British tourists arrested in Benidorm after fight with locals.	two British tourists local people		
WELL SCOOTED! 81-year-old Taunton granddad's 650-mile, three-day journey to see daughters.			
CRASH COURSE IN DRIVING LEAVES A TRAIL OF DESTRUCTION Teenager's first and last time at the wheel.			
PUPILS PROVE POINT Buses back in High Wigley after primary school children teach council officials a thing or two.			

Teachers' note Using the first example, model how to read a headline for clues as to what the story is about: ask the children what happened and where, and what kind of people were involved. Ask them to think about whom the headline suggests were the main participants in the incident.

Developing Literacy
Non-fiction Year 4
© A & C Black 2002

What's the story? 2

- **Write the headline for this newspaper story.**

A grey horse stands tied to a post beside the village green in High Wigley. The post is part of an old bus stop, but no buses have been seen in this tiny hamlet for more than 15 years.

"This is the only way I can come and see my friends here," said 15-year-old Clare, the horse's rider.

Anyone without a horse, bike or car has to rely on taxis or lifts from neighbours.

But that's about to change, thanks to the 14 pupils at the village school. "The children asked me why no buses came here," said headteacher Mary Patel, 36. "I said, 'Why don't you write to the council?', and that is just what they did."

Jake Marks, 10, was puzzled by the council's reply. It said that the roads leading to the village were too narrow for buses, but he knew about the old bus stop. He and the other pupils interviewed older residents, who remembered buses coming to the village.

Jake also asked his father, Mike, 39, a coach driver in nearby Low Wigley, to try driving his coach to High Wigley. He found the roads plenty wide enough.

The council has agreed to start a bus service to High Wigley from next month.

- **Make notes about the main points of the story.**

No buses to or from High Wigley

- **Compare these with your notes in *What's the story? 1*.**

- **Find six newspaper stories.**
- **Predict the stories from the headlines, then read the stories.**
- **Compare your predictions with the stories.**

Teachers' note The children should first complete the activity on page 14 and have it to refer to. Encourage them to skim-read the story, then match it to one of the headlines on the chart. They could begin by underlining the key phrases and sentences. When comparing their notes, they should comment on how well they predicted the story and how well the headline and sub-heading introduced it.

Developing Literacy
Non-fiction Year 4
© A & C Black 2002

Read all about it!

- **Read the newspaper article.**
- **Label the different parts of it.**

- direct speech
- headline
- indirect speech
- opening sentence
- paragraph to explain the story
- photograph
- simple description
- sub-heading
- cross-heading

headline

PRINCE'S SEARCH FOR MISS TINY TOES

Posh shoe Archie's only souvenir of palace disco

The Queen held a disco at the palace last night to celebrate Prince Archie's eighteenth birthday.

A throng of no fewer than a hundred youngsters spent the evening dancing in the palace ballroom, but Prince Archie had eyes only for the girl in the posh blue dress and even posher shoes. "She was the cleverest and wittiest girl I have ever met, and she knew more about cricket than any of the others," sighed Archie. Rupert Hyphen-Jones, 16, who was also at the disco, nodded in agreement and added, "She is also an expert on Harry Potter."

In Prince Archie's hand was a tiny designer shoe of the poshest quality. The shoe has a cream leather sole and blue leather uppers, and there is a small blue bow on the front. The most remarkable thing about the shoe is its size – a minuscule 12. Few girls of eighteen could have feet so tiny.

Midnight flit

How did the girl come to leave her shoe behind? Prince Archie said that she had suddenly looked at the clock, noticed it was midnight, shrieked and run off. He added that she muttered something about a pumpkin and that he tripped over two lizards and four mice as he ran after her.

Palace officials will call at every household whose census form includes a girl of eighteen.

- **Explain the purpose of each part of the newspaper article.**

**Developing Literacy
Non-fiction Year 4
© A & C Black 2002**

Formal or informal?

- **Read these newspaper articles.**
- **Write** formal **or** informal **in the boxes.**

1.

It's going to be chilly today and there's a chance it might rain. So take a brolly out with you, but watch out – it could be blowy. The highest temperature will be 11° Celsius – a bit on the low side for June.

2.

The villagers of Much Sniffton are becoming increasingly annoyed by the presence of film crews. Locals complain that their streets are blocked by trucks and that their everyday life is disrupted when traffic is removed from the cobbled square, and when anything which looks too modern is hidden.

3.

Film crews are bugging the villagers of Much Sniffton. They don't want trucks blocking the streets and they don't like it when they can't drive through the square. They are even more miffed when the film crews hide anything which looks too modern.

4.

Temperatures today will not rise above 11° Celsius, which is below average for June. There is a possibility of rain and gusts of wind.

- **Which features can be found in each article? Write examples.**

Article number	Passive verbs	Contractions	Everyday expressions	Speaking directly to the reader as 'you'
1	–	It's	brolly	
2				
3				
4				

- **Explain how you can tell whether a newspaper article is formal or informal.**

Formal articles ____

____

____

Informal articles ____

____

____

Teachers' note To introduce the activity, read out formal and informal passages from newspapers and ask the children to identify them as formal or informal. Discuss the differences between the two, noting active/passive verbs, the use of contractions and everyday phrases used in speech, and direct references to the reader.

Developing Literacy
Non-fiction Year 4
© A & C Black 2002

Instructions test

- **Read different kinds of** instructions .
- **Record what you notice about them.**

Title of instructions	What the instructions are for	Where the instructions come from	Features of the instructions (✓ or ✗)				
			The aim is stated at the start	List of equipment/ materials	Step-by-step order	Imperative verbs	Diagrams

- **Choose one of the sets of instructions.**
- **Write an evaluation of it.**

What made the instructions easy or difficult to follow?

Teachers' note The children need access to a collection of instructions of different types: for example, instructions for using equipment or making models, recipes, rules for games or *The Highway Code*. They can be printed or electronic and can include illustrations, captions and labels.

Developing Literacy
Non-fiction Year 4
© A & C Black 2002

Electronic text review

- **Use this page to** review **an ICT text you have used.**

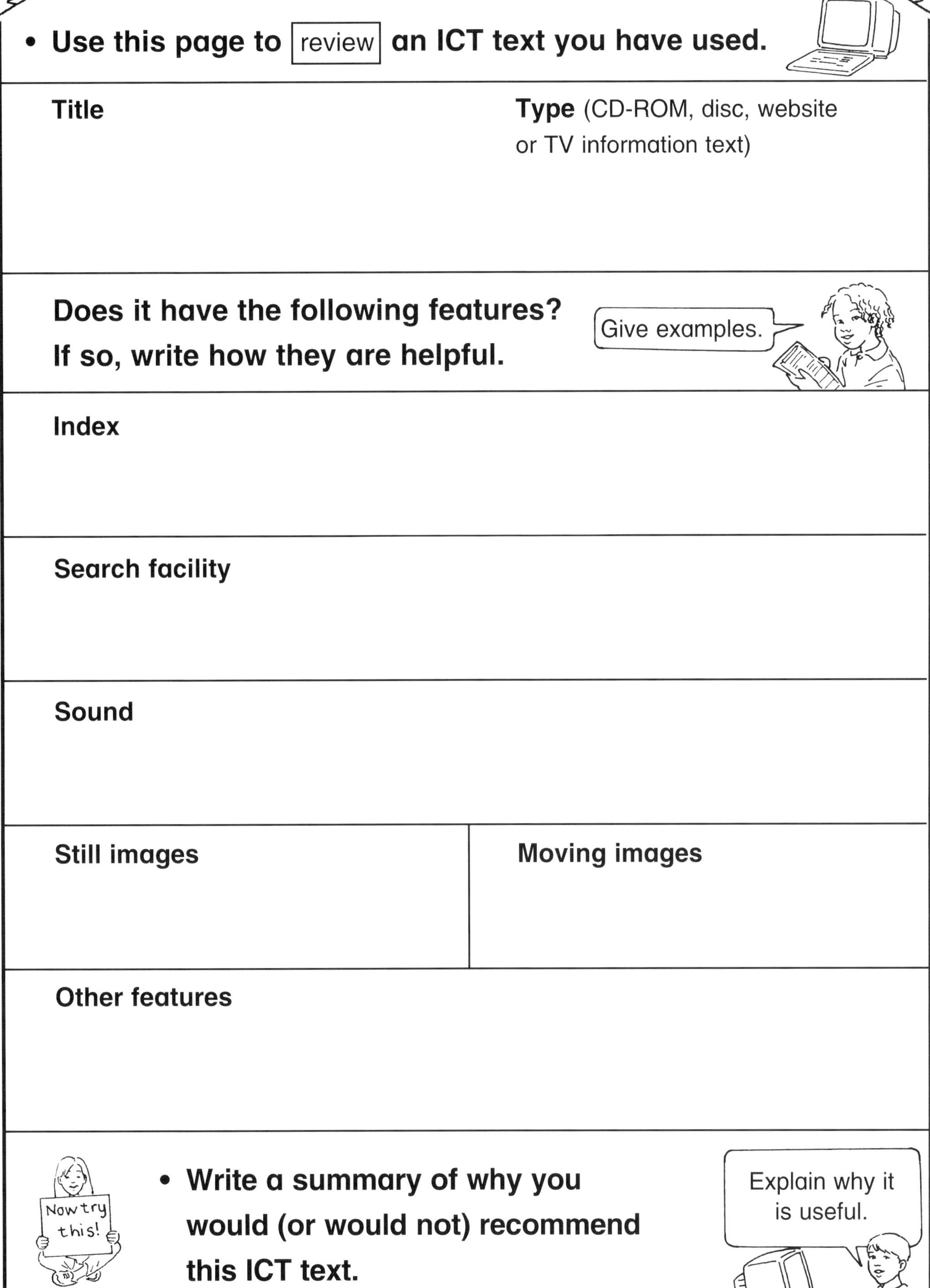

Title	**Type** (CD-ROM, disc, website or TV information text)

Does it have the following features? If so, write how they are helpful.

Index

Search facility

Sound

Still images	**Moving images**

Other features

- **Write a summary of why you would (or would not) recommend this ICT text.**

Teachers' note Different groups could review different types of electronic text (including CD-ROMs, discs, television text services and websites). Discuss some of the features of the texts and whether they help the reader to find and understand information.

**Developing Literacy
Non-fiction Year 4**
© A & C Black 2002

Ready for research

What would you like to find out?

- **Use this page to prepare for your research and to record what you find out.**

My question

____

The sources I shall use:

books _________________________   places _________________________

_________________________   _________________________

CD-ROMs _________________________   people _________________________

_________________________   _________________________

websites _________________________   other _________________________

_________________________   _________________________

I found out ____

____

____

I could not find out _________________________________

____

The most useful sources were _________________________

____

____

____

Developing Literacy
Non-fiction Year 4
© A & C Black 2002

Will it help?

- **Use this page to help you choose the most useful texts for your research.**
- **What do you want to find out?** _______________________
- **Choose some texts which might help you.**
- **Scan the texts, looking at the contents page, index and headings.**
- **Make notes on the chart about each text.**

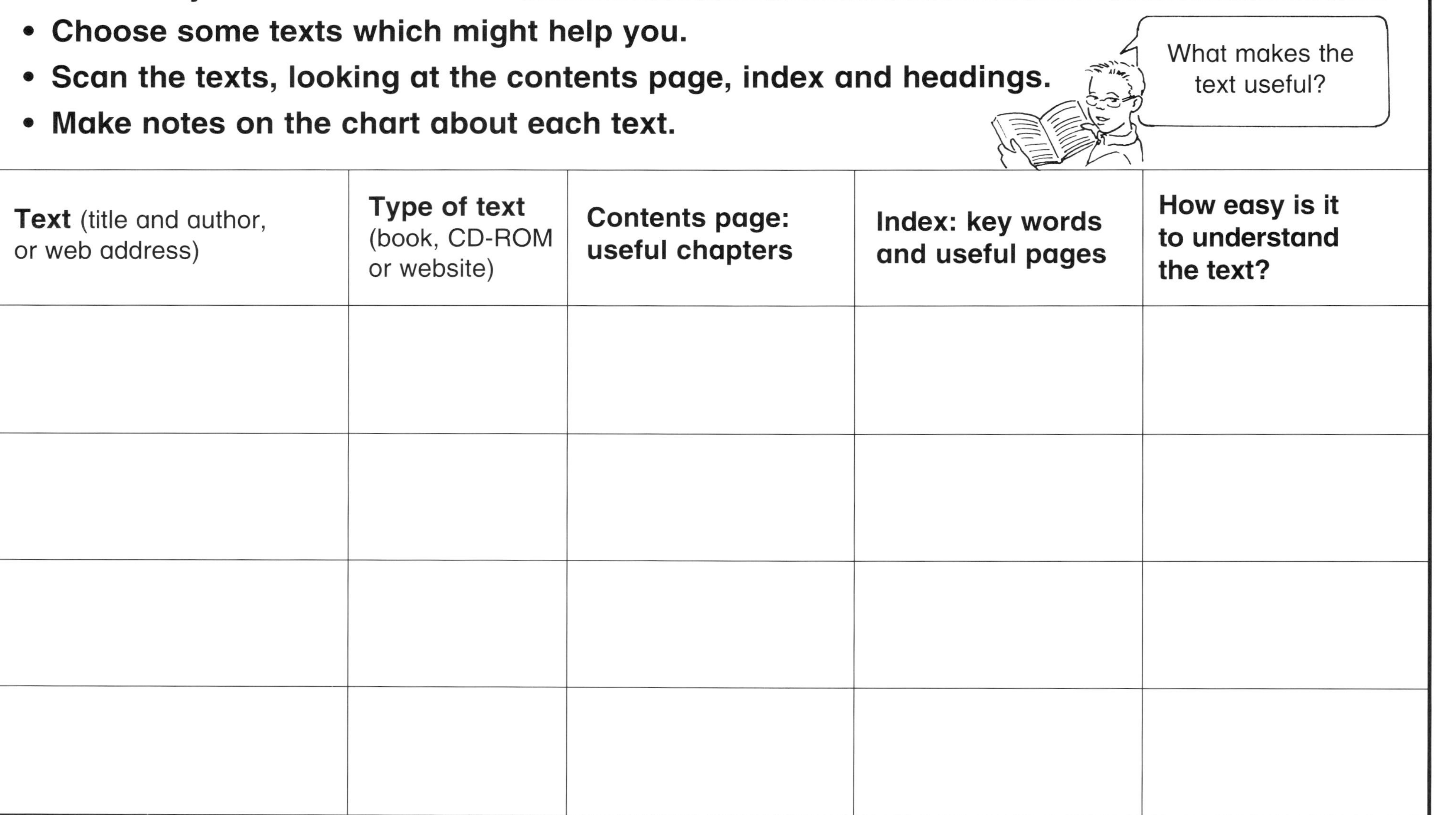

Text (title and author, or web address)	**Type of text** (book, CD-ROM or website)	**Contents page: useful chapters**	**Index: key words and useful pages**	**How easy is it to understand the text?**

Developing Literacy
Non-fiction Year 4
© A & C Black 2002

Is it clear?

- **Read the information about hedgehogs.**
- **Underline any words you do not understand.**

Hedgehogs are a suburban success story. In our gardens, parks and cemeteries they have found welcome relief from the changing face of agriculture. They have effective strategies for survival, threatened mainly by the ravages of winter and the thoughtlessness of people.

These mammals, whose ancestors roamed the earth before mammoths and sabre-toothed tigers, have changed little over the last 15 million years. Like many of the first mammals they have adapted to a nocturnal, insectivorous way of life. They eat at least 100 invertebrates per night – favourites on the menu are beetles, caterpillars and earthworms, supplemented by slugs and even pet food. Relying on a strong sense of smell, which can detect prey up to three centimetres underground, they wander through their habitat, foraging for food and covering a distance of about two miles each night.

- **Complete the chart.**

Word	What I think it means	Clues in the text	The dictionary definition

Continue on another sheet of paper if necessary.

- **Write out any sentences you do not understand.**
- **Work out what each one might mean.**
- **Check in a dictionary.**
- **Re-write the text in simpler language.**

Teachers' note You could begin by explaining that the information text on this page is quite difficult to understand, and that when the children come across parts of a text which they find difficult, they should stop and check any new words and re-read any difficult sentences.

Developing Literacy
Non-fiction Year 4
© A & C Black 2002

Summary match

The paragraphs of this text are in the wrong order.

- **Match the paragraphs to the summaries.**
- **Put the paragraphs and summaries in the correct order.**
- **Glue them on to a chart.**

Paragraphs

The Romans came back to Britain for the third time in AD 43 with a huge army of about 40,000 soldiers led by their emperor, Claudius. The Britons could not keep them out. The Romans captured many villages.

The Romans ruled Colchester. Many of the Britons there were happy because they had everything they needed. Roman soldiers were given land in Colchester, but some of them wanted more; they began driving the Britons off their land.

Julius Caesar led the first Roman visit to Britain in 55 BC to find out about this land on the edge of the world. He left after a few weeks, but came back a year later with a bigger army. He captured land in the south.

When the Britons saw Romans landing on their shores for the first time, they got ready for battle. They dyed their skin blue with a plant called woad and put lime on their hair to make it stand up on end.

The greed of the Roman soldiers and the cruel way in which they began to treat the Britons made the Britons want to rebel.

Claudius' army captured Colchester in AD 43. They built a great city there, which they called Camulodunum, and made it their capital in Britain.

Summaries

Problems between the Romans and the Britons.	The Romans' third visit to Britain, led by Claudius.
The Romans' first two visits to Britain led by Julius Caesar.	The Britons prepare for battle.
Life in Colchester under the Romans.	The Romans capture Colchester.

Teachers' note Once the children have put the paragraphs in order, ask them to read the text and check that it makes sense. They could also cut up other texts into paragraphs, write summaries of the paragraphs and then mix up the paragraphs and summaries for a friend to re-order.

Developing Literacy
Non-fiction Year 4
© A & C Black 2002

An explanation

- **Read the** explanation.

How birds fly

The shape and structure of a bird's body help it to fly.

If a bird were too heavy for the strength of its wings, it would not be able to fly. Birds are light because their bones are hollow (the spaces inside them are filled with air).

Birds whose wings are small compared with their bodies cannot fly well: for example, hens (and penguins, which cannot fly at all). Most birds' wings are very strong so that when they flap their wings they rise into the air.

The shape of a bird's body is streamlined, which means that air passes easily over and under it. This helps the bird to glide through the air. The wings are shaped like an aerofoil – rounded on the top and curved upwards underneath. This shape makes air pass quickly over the top of the wings. Fast-moving air pushes downwards less than slow-moving air does, and so the birds' wings are lifted.

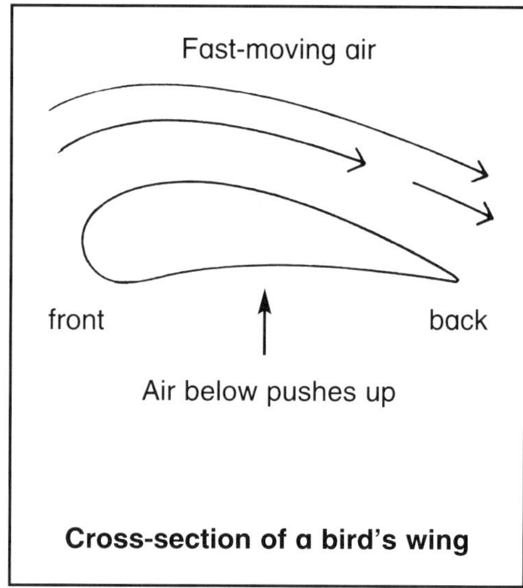

- ## Summarise the text.

This text explains _______________________________

It begins by _______________________________

____

It goes on to _______________________________

____

____

Then it _______________________________

____

Finally it _______________________________

____

Teachers' note It will be useful if the children first complete the activity on page 23. You could begin by asking them what 'explanation' means. Ask them which other word it reminds them of ('explain'), and point out that this is what an explanation does – it explains how something happens, how something works or how something can be done.

Developing Literacy
Non-fiction Year 4
© A & C Black 2002

Features of explanations

- **Use this page to help you describe the features of an explanation.**

Title

Purpose of explanation

Structure   Does it have:

a)   an introduction? ☐   b)   a step-by-step sequence? ☐

c)   a separate paragraph for each step? ☐

d)   illustrations? ☐   e)   diagrams? ☐

Language features   Give examples of:

- **Read some other explanations.**
- **Record your findings.**

Teachers' note The children should first complete the activity on page 24 and have it available to refer to. It will be useful to discuss what is meant by 'a step-by-step sequence' and 'a separate paragraph for each step'. You might also need to revise present tense, passive voice, connectives of time and cause and effect.

Developing Literacy
Non-fiction Year 4
© A & C Black 2002

Arguments: 1

An argument gives the writer's own point of view.
- **Write a heading to say what each argument is about.**
- **Write a sentence to sum up what the writer thinks.**

Heading __________________

Green Lane is not safe for pedestrians or cyclists. A footpath and cycle path are needed. We should be encouraged to walk or cycle without fear of traffic. Many children who live close enough to school to walk or cycle there have to go by car because of the danger of traffic in Green Lane. Moreover, several cyclists have been hurt in accidents with cars.

Summary

Heading __________________

Anyone whose dog attacks delivery people should have a mailbox and an intercom at the gate to their home. This would save anyone delivering mail or other goods from injury by vicious dogs. In addition to giving delivery people personal safety, it would save money. The Post Office wastes thousands of pounds through lost time when its workers are attending hospitals or recovering from dog bites.

Summary

Heading __________________

It would be good to have the school year split into four terms instead of three. The summer holiday is too long; we forget much of what we have learned during the six-week break. If this break were shortened, there would be no need to spend so much time on revision every September. More importantly for people of different religions, there could be holidays for the different festivals. This would be fair to everyone.

Summary

Heading __________________

Schools should have anti-bullying practice along with fire-drill and road safety practice. Fire-drill helps us to learn what to do in the event of a fire, just as the *Green Cross Code* helps us to act safely when crossing roads. Bullies make many children miserable. If we practised what to do when bullied, we would be better prepared if it really happened.

Summary

Teachers' note You could begin by asking the children for a definition of an argument, in case they think that it implies enmity, aggression or even a fight. Explain that an argument gives a point of view supported by evidence. Model the first example, encouraging the children to think up headings and summaries which are as brief as possible.

Developing Literacy
Non-fiction Year 4
© A & C Black 2002

Arguments: 2

- **Read what the people say.**
- **Decide whether there should be public paths across private land.**
- **Write notes for your argument.**

The reasons for having public footpaths across private land are

____

____

This might not be welcome to landowners because ____________

____

____

I think ___________________________________

____

Teachers' note It is useful to discuss the meanings of 'for', 'against', 'support' and 'oppose'. The children could work in pairs or small groups to discuss points which could be made to support or oppose the argument.

**Developing Literacy
Non-fiction Year 4**
© A & C Black 2002

Structure an argument

- **Cut out the sentences and put them in order to make an argument.**
- **Use the words from the list to link the sentences.**
- **Check that your argument still makes sense.**

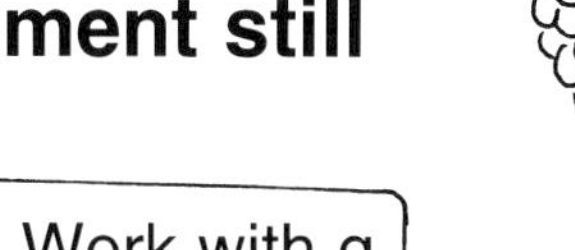

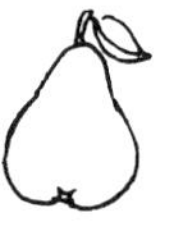

Logical connectives

after all
also
as well as that
because
for example
however
if
in order to
moreover
nonetheless
so
therefore

A different type of fruit should be provided for them each day. 

Some children do not eat breakfast.

Experts say that we should try to eat five portions of fruit or vegetables a day.

Fruit and vegetables contain many vitamins, minerals and fibres, which are all essential for good health.

Different fruits contain different vitamins and minerals. 

Some children would not otherwise have the chance to eat fruit.

The government should pay for schools to give all pupils a piece of fruit each day.

Fruit and vegetables with deep orange, green or red colours help the body to produce vitamin A.

Eating fruit rather than sweets as a snack is better for the teeth. 

A mid-morning snack of fruit would help to stop tiredness caused by hunger.

Teachers' note The children should first complete the activities on pages 26 and 27 and should have read and discussed some argument texts (for example, from magazines and newspapers). Point out the order in which an argument is structured and ensure that the children understand the logical connectives on the page.

**Developing Literacy
Non-fiction Year 4
© A & C Black 2002**

28

A discussion

A discussion is different from an argument.
A discussion gives many different views.

- **Read the discussion.**

Use a dictionary.

Some people think that children under the age of ten should be banned from being out without adults after 6 p.m. They say that unsupervised children annoy people by their unruly behaviour and that it is not safe for them to be out alone in the evening.

Shopkeepers say many of the thefts they suffer are carried out by children and that a curfew would cut down petty crime: "I'm not saying that all youngsters out on their own are up to no good, but some of them are, and they're the ones we want to stop," said one shopkeeper. Several people agreed with this, and said that if children are not doing anything wrong, why should they object to being supervised?

On the other hand, most children under the age of ten do not cause any trouble. Why should they suffer because of the few who do? Moreover, some irresponsible adults break the law, while many ten-year-olds are sensible enough to take responsibility for their own safety and behaviour without having to be supervised, whatever the time of the day.

Another important point is that children should be encouraged to take responsibility for their own behaviour. If they can be trusted to behave sensibly, they do not need to be watched over all the time.

- **Write on the chart the different views.**

For a ban	Against a ban
Unsupervised children annoy people	

- **List the verbs in the discussion.**
- **Write the verb tense next to each verb.**
- **List the logical connectives used.**

Teachers' note The children should first have completed the activities on pages 26 to 28. You could read the text with them and ask them to look for similarities and differences between this and the other arguments they have read.

Developing Literacy
Non-fiction Year 4
© A & C Black 2002

Persuasion

- ## Read this page from a leaflet.

Sunshine Fun Beach is a unique collection of entertainment attractions designed to provide enjoyment for everyone. From our famous Cosmic Dayglo Bowling to tennis, from state-of-the-art virtual reality games to traditional fairground stalls and rides, the choice is yours every day of the year.

Weather is never a problem here at Sunshine Fun Beach: most of the attractions are indoors and many are covered by sliding all-weather roofs, which can be opened to let in sunshine and closed to keep out rain and snow.

Transport is no problem. We have acres of parking, an excellent bus service and a hi-tech monorail system. In the larger buildings there are escalators and 'people-movers' for our less active visitors.

Bring the whole family for an affordable fun day out. You can picnic at a lakeside table, savour the delights of a top-class restaurant or grab a quick but delicious and wholesome snack at a 'Beach Bites' cafe.

- ## List the facts you can find about Sunshine Fun Beach.

It has bowling, tennis,

- ## On the chart, list the adjectives from the leaflet.

Adjectives giving information	Adjectives which persuade

- ## Underline all the positive adjectives.
- ## Re-write the leaflet page, changing all the adjectives to their opposites. What effect does this have?

Teachers' note The children could compare the text on this page with information texts such as explanations, reports and recounts. They should notice that this text gives information in a way which encourages people to visit the place.

Developing Literacy
Non-fiction Year 4
© A & C Black 2002

Come and buy!

- **Read the** advertisement .

- **Complete the chart.**

Examples of advertisement features		
Adjectives crunchiest	**Alliteration**	**Jingles**
Invented words	**Scientific language**	**Special offers**

- **Write about how the advertisement attracts people's attention.**

How does it suggest that *Crackles* crisps and the people who eat them are special?

Teachers' note The children should first read examples of real advertisements; you could read them as shared texts. Discuss the purpose of advertisements, and ask the children to identify the audience of each one (and to say how they can they tell). Ask them to consider how the advertisement attracts attention and how it makes people want to buy the product.

**Developing Literacy
Non-fiction Year 4
© A & C Black 2002**

Target practice

- **Summarise each paragraph in a sentence with as few words as possible.**

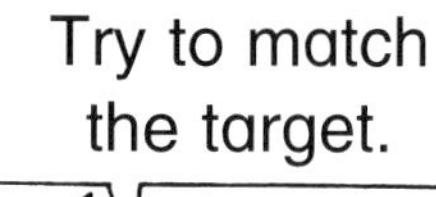

Three quarters of the class would like to have a shorter afternoon break and finish school earlier. A quarter of the class disagree with this. They do not want to change.	A competition was held in the village to find the fastest runner.

Three quarters of the class would like to have a shorter afternoon break and finish school earlier. A quarter of the class disagree with this. They do not want to change.

A competition was held in the village to find the fastest runner.

5

13

There was an old woman who lived in a shoe. She had seventeen children. She had ten daughters and seven sons.

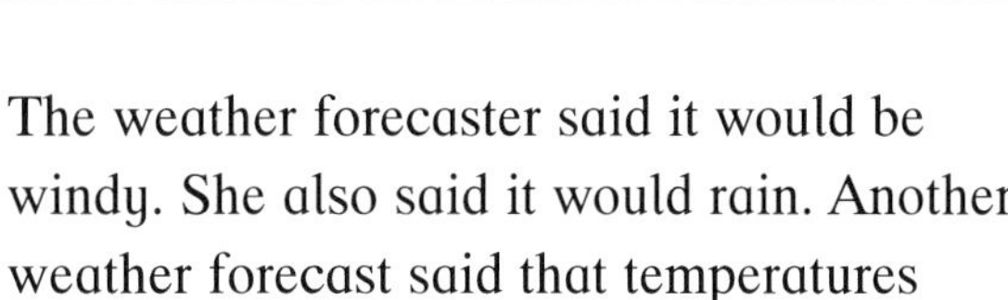

The weather forecaster said it would be windy. She also said it would rain. Another weather forecast said that temperatures would be low.

12

At the fancy dress party some children dressed as animals. There were also children dressed as clowns and fairies.

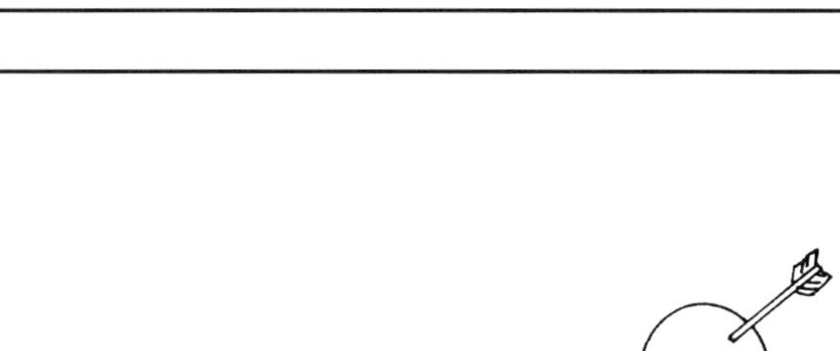

7

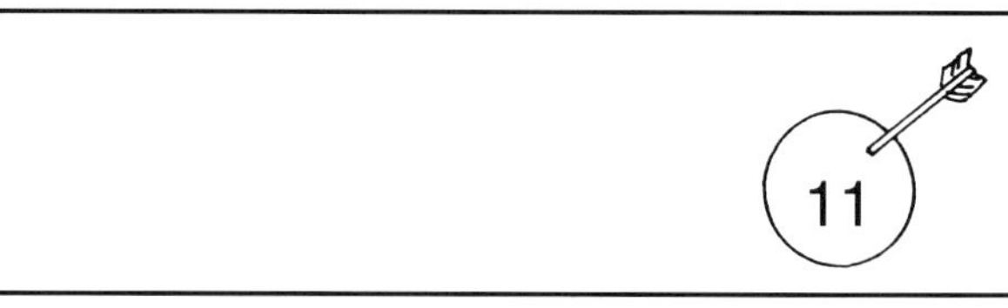

11

- **Re-read some of your own written work.**
- **Write a summary of each piece of writing.**

Teachers' note Discuss ways in which sentences can be combined by using connectives (including 'which' and 'who'), changing active sentences to the passive, experimenting with changing verbs to nouns or vice versa and combining information. You could model the first example: 'Most of the class want a shorter afternoon break and an earlier finish.'

Developing Literacy
Non-fiction Year 4
© A & C Black 2002

Write all about it!

- **Plan a newspaper article about an event in your family.**

Headline

Sub-heading

1. Introduction

2. Details

3. Quotes

4. Extra information

5. Cross-headings

6. Summary

- **Use your notes to help you write your newspaper article.**

- **Draw a picture to go with the article.**

Teachers' note It will be helpful if the children have first completed pages 14 to 16. You could begin by asking them to describe briefly any events in their families. These can be ordinary, everyday happenings, but the children can aim to write about them in an interesting way. It will be useful to model how to write the articles.

**Developing Literacy
Non-fiction Year 4
© A & C Black 2002**

Make it fit: 1

The articles for the school newspaper do not fit into the spaces on the page.

- Edit the articles.
- **Cross out in red any parts which are not necessary.**
- **Underline in blue the most important parts.**
- **Re-write the articles.**

BEN FINDS HIS FEET
First day at nursery poses problems for my little brother

It was the day my mum had been looking forward to for three years. Shopping was going to be so easy, and she could even wear her favourite jeans without fear of squashed biscuits. The whole family had taken turns to help Ben learn all the new things he would have to do for himself once he went to nursery. I showed him how to fasten buttons; I practised with him every night. He would begin from the middle, but there was usually at least one button or buttonhole too many when he got to the end! I showed him how to start at one end instead of in the middle. Mum helped him to do up zips; she let him do a bit more for himself each day.

At the end of Ben's first morning at the nursery, he came rushing out to show Mum how he had done up his buttons and his zip – but his feet seemed to be pointing in the wrong directions! There is something else we need to practise with Ben!

By Katie Smith, Class 4a

Teachers' note This could be used with page 35 to help the children write a class newspaper. They could first look at some newspapers featuring several short articles on one page, and discuss the way in which text is organised to fit into the available space. Explain that if a piece is too long, it should not be shortened by merely cutting out the part at the end that does not fit. Continued on page 35.

Developing Literacy
Non-fiction Year 4
© A & C Black 2002

Make it fit: 2

SURPRISE BIRTHDAY PARTY
What we did for my dad

We had been planning Dad's surprise party for months. We wanted to make his fortieth birthday special. It was amazing that he didn't hear us whispering. He never seemed to notice that we would suddenly stop talking when he came into a room.

When the day came the whole family arrived at our house. There were about 20 people: my grandmothers, grandfathers, aunts, uncles, cousins and some of Dad's friends. We had all clubbed together to buy a present for him, and there it was, all wrapped up on the table next to the cake with its 40 candles. We wondered where Dad was. He was much later than usual coming home from work. After a while the phone rang. It was Dad. He said that he had just remembered that it was his birthday, and that he wanted to see if the family and his friends could come to our house and celebrate it with him. He had been trying to phone everyone, but for some reason no one seemed to be at home.

Mum was trying to think of a way to get him to come home without telling him what was going on, but she couldn't. Then everyone started singing 'Happy birthday to you!'

By Curtis Jones, Class 5b

125 words

- **Write some instructions for editing text to make it shorter.**

Teachers' note Continued from page 34. The children could key in the texts and edit them on screen, using the word-processor's word-count facility to check the number of words.

Developing Literacy
Non-fiction Year 4
© A & C Black 2002

Writing instructions

Instructions tell the reader how to make or do something.

- **Use this page to help you write some instructions.**

Purpose	Equipment and materials

Step 1

Step 2

Step 3

Step 4

- **Write your instructions in full. Include diagrams and illustrations.**
- **Ask a friend to check the instructions for sense.**
- **List the good points about your instructions.**
- **Make a note of what can be improved.**

Teachers' note The children first need to read examples of different types of instructions. It will be helpful if they have also completed the activity on page 18. Discuss the ways in which connectives, such as those in the word-bank, can be used to link the steps into which the instructions are split. Also discuss the layout features which help the reader to follow the steps in the correct order.

**Developing Literacy
Non-fiction Year 4
© A & C Black 2002**

Keep it short

When you write notes, you usually need to write quickly. You need to understand the notes when you read them again.

- **Make notes about the passage.**

You might have looked at the specks of lights in the night sky and wondered about them. You know, of course, that they are stars, but do you know what a star is?

Stars look small from the Earth because of their great distance from it. The ones you can see are many times bigger than the Earth. The Sun is a star and, like the other stars, it is an enormous ball of burning gases.

A star forms when gas and dust from space collect, pulled together by gravity. The dust and gases burn and shrink, and as they do so they become hotter. The temperature of a star can be as high as 16 million degrees Celsius. This heat creates light. On Earth we cannot feel the heat of any stars except the Sun, because they are too far away.

Stars can be different colours. The hottest are blue, white ones are cooler, then yellow and then red.

- **Swap notes with a friend.**
- **Use the notes to write an information text.**
- **Compare your text with the one on this page.**

Teachers' note You could begin by modelling the process of making notes: 'think aloud' about the words and phrases you think need to be recorded, explaining why and how you can record them as briefly as possible.

Developing Literacy
Non-fiction Year 4
© A & C Black 2002

The children made notes from different sources about the Second World War.

Covered windows – Thick black curtains
No light must show – light gave bombers
                        target at night.

No bananas or other foreign foods –
no ships getting here.

Food rationed – had to give in coupons.
per week : 50g margarine , 3½ pints
per person   of milk, 100g cheese,
              350g meat.

Children in Liverpool sent to Wales to
be safe.

Interview with Lisa's gran

Wartime rations
Each adult – 3 eggs (not fresh,
              dried powder)
        50g butter
        75g sweets
        50g jam
        50g cooking fat

People told – eat home-grown
veg. like potato, carrot.

Potato + carrot recipes on
radio each day.
'The War in Britain' by J. Joy
      Better Publishing 1960

Clothes + materials rationed.
'Make do and mend'
Women's mags full of ideas for re-using
old clothes.
No stockings – women dyed legs with
'leg tan' or gravy browning.
U.S. soldiers brought nylon stockings
– gifts for girls.
'Wartime Wardrobes' by C.M. Smith, Red Books.
                                      1998

1939 children (school age) sent to
countryside. Families had to take
them in.
Trains from cities (Liverpool, London,
Birmingham, Leeds, Coventry) to country.
Labels on coats – name, address, school.

'Britain Since 1930', John Corn, Folens, 1994

Air raid shelter in
garden.
Made of metal.
Covered top with
soil and turf.
Safe – no glass no
heavy weight to
fall.

Interview with
Rick's grandad.

Developing Literacy
Non-fiction Year 4
© A & C Black 2002

Different sources: 2

- **Use this chart to organise the notes about the Second World War.**

Effects of the Second World War on daily life

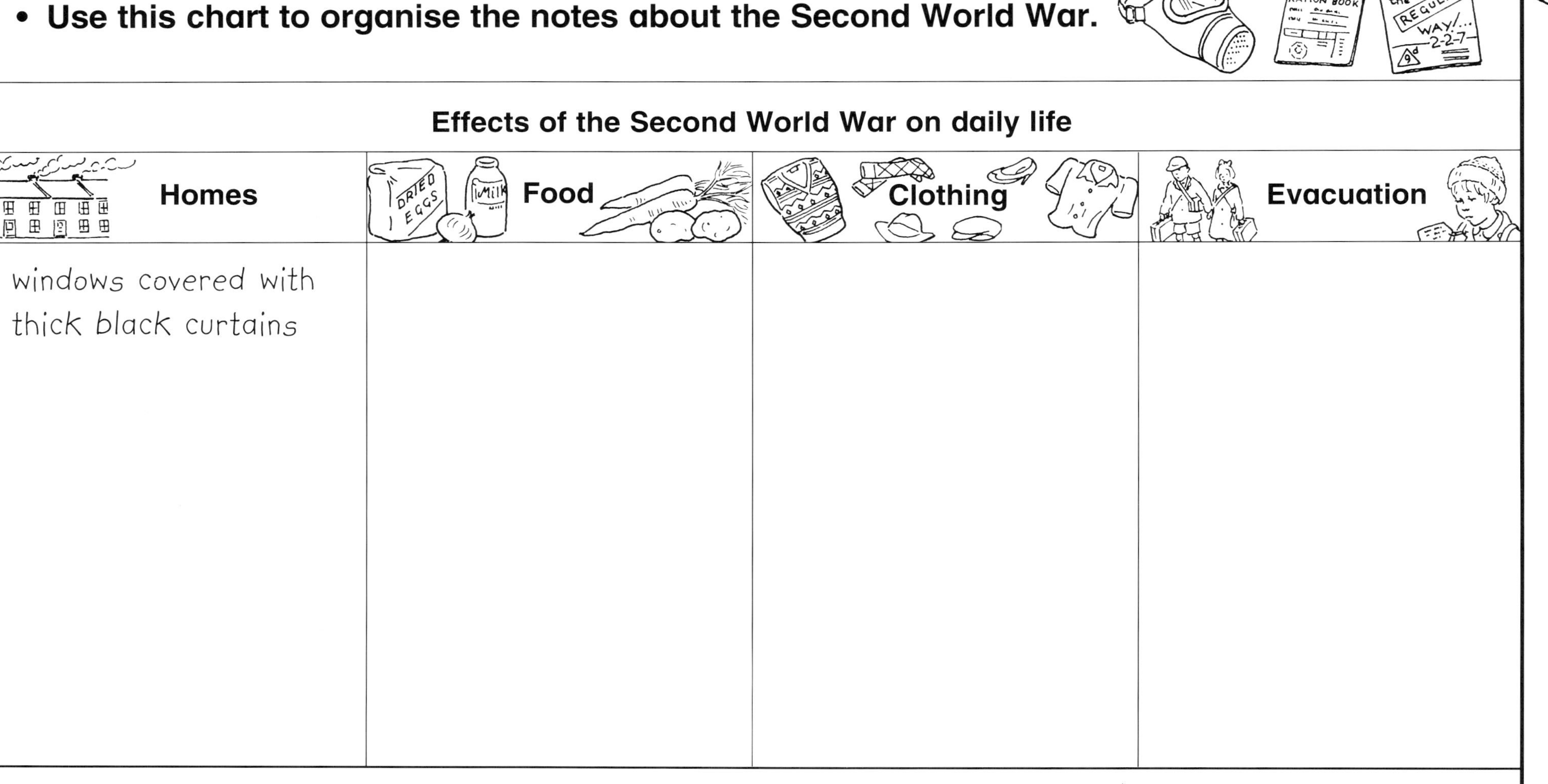

Homes	Food	Clothing	Evacuation
windows covered with thick black curtains			

- **Make notes from different sources about a topic you are studying.**
  You could use as sources:
- **Use a chart to organise your notes.**   older people   books   CD-ROMs   websites

---

Teachers' note Continued from page 38. Make clear to the children how a chart can be useful for organising notes from various sources on different, but related, topics; the notes made from each source are sometimes about several topics and it is useful to separate them out.

Developing Literacy
Non-fiction Year 4
© A & C Black 2002

From notes to sentences

- **Read the fact-file about the city of Carlisle.**
- **Use the information to write a report.**

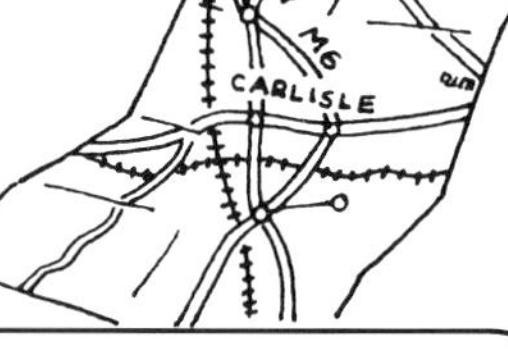

CARLISLE

Site: NW England. Nr Solway Firth, where R. Eden meets R.Caldew. N. end of M6 motorway.

Roman settlement (Luguvallium). Roman walls. Tully House Museum – Roman items. Near to Hadrian's Wall and Housesteads Roman Fort.

Settle—Carlisle Railway (Victorian, 1865)

Cathedral (rebuilt in 1492). **Castle** – first built 1092 (wood). Later rebuilt in stone (12th century).

Football team – Carlisle United. Div 3. Bruton Park.

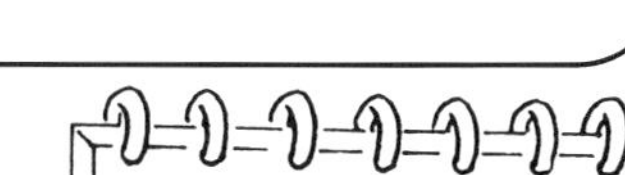

Report

Carlisle, in North-West England, is situated

____

____

____

____

____

____

____

____

Continue on another sheet of paper.

Useful words

Verbs
are, can, is, see

Adjectives
ancient, historic, modern, old

Connectives
also, and, at, beside, but, by, in, near, nearby, next to

- **Compare your report with a friend's.**
- **Edit and change your report to improve it.**

Teachers' note Discuss with the class the way in which the notes are written. Point out the abbreviations and ask the children if they know what they all represent. Ask them to supply any missing words and to explain why they have been missed out.

**Developing Literacy
Non-fiction Year 4
© A & C Black 2002**

Notes on a diagram

- **Read the information about the Greek goddess Athena.**
- **Record the main points on the diagram.**

Athena was the daughter of Zeus and Metis. Zeus had swallowed Metis to stop her giving birth to a son who might be more powerful than himself. The god Hephaestus cut open the forehead of Zeus and out sprang Athena.

Zeus made Athena and the god Ares the patrons of warfare: Athena was good at planning battles and Ares enjoyed fighting. Athena helped the Greeks to win many battles against the Trojans.

Together Athena and the god Poseidon took over the land of Attica. The gods asked them to make gifts to the people there. Athena gave an olive tree and Poseidon gave a horse. The gods judged Athena's gift to be the more useful. They made her patron of Athens and all cities.

Athena invented the flute and became the patron of arts and handicrafts in cities and the goddess of wisdom. A great temple, the Acropolis, was built for her on the Parthenon, a hill in Athens.

Birth

Parents
Father: Zeus   Mother: Metis

Skills and talents

Links with other gods and goddesses

Athena

Achievements

Special honours

- **Read about a character from history. Make notes on a diagram.**

Teachers' note Enlarge the page to A3 if the children need more space. Read the headings on the diagram and model how to find information connected with each heading. After completing the extension activity, the children could use their notes as the basis for a report.

Developing Literacy
Non-fiction Year 4
© A & C Black 2002

How does it work?

- **This is a cat-feeding machine.**

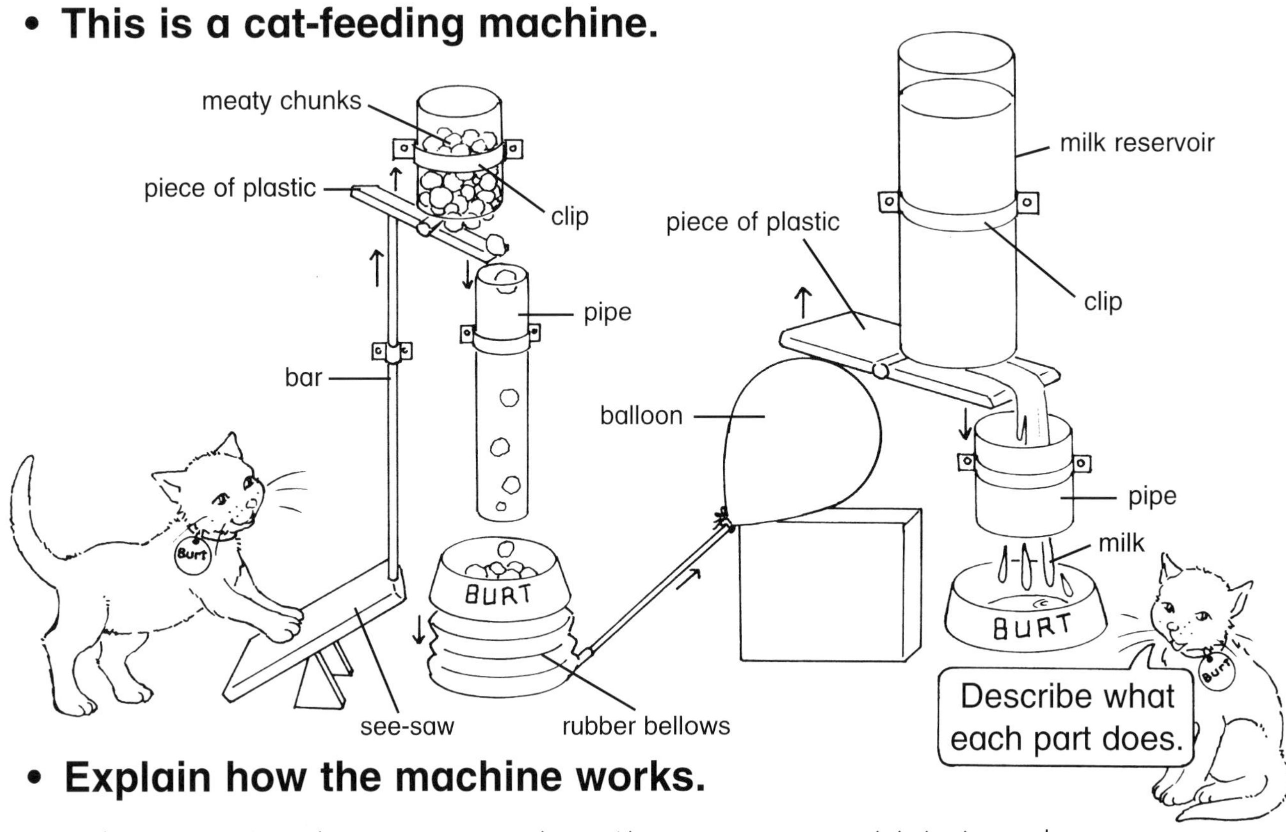

- **Explain how the machine works.**

1. The cat stands on one end of the see-saw, which is a lever.

2. The other end of the see-saw goes up. _______________________

____

____

____

____

____

____

Continue on another sheet of paper.

- **Design your own machine. Draw a diagram.**
- **Write a caption to say what it is for.**
- **Explain how the machine works.**

Teachers' note You could begin by discussing what is happening in the picture. Ask the children to identify the starting point of the process, what happens next and so on. Point out the importance of writing an explanation in the correct order. The children should notice that an explanation is written in the present tense and the third person.

Developing Literacy
Non-fiction Year 4
© A & C Black 2002

For and against

- **Read what people said to a reporter.**

- **Colour red the outlines of the speeches which support the railway.**
- **Colour blue the outlines of the speeches which oppose it.**
- **Plan an argument <u>either</u> to support <u>or</u> to oppose the railway.**

Teachers' note Use this with page 44. It will be helpful if the children have first completed the activities on pages 26 to 28. You could begin by discussing what the people say, noting that each speech is in two parts: it gives a statement followed by evidence in support.

Developing Literacy
Non-fiction Year 4
© A & C Black 2002

Plan an argument

Problem	
My point of view	
The points I shall make	**Evidence to support these points**
1.	
2.	
3.	
4.	

Conclusion

- **Write an argument based on your notes.**

according to	because	in addition	so
as a result of	besides	moreover	therefore
as well	however	since	thus

Teachers' note Use this with page 43. Begin by asking the children what the argument is about ('Problem') and then to say which point of view they support ('My point of view'). After that they should enter the statements which agree with their point of view and the evidence to support each one. The conclusion should repeat their point of view.

Developing Literacy
Non-fiction Year 4
© A & C Black 2002

A letter to argue

- **Re-write an argument as a letter to a newspaper.**

Write your address. ⟶ ______________________

Write the date. ⟶ ______________________

Dear Editor,

I think that ______________________ ⟵ State your point of view.
____
____

I have several reasons for thinking this. — Give evidence for each statement.
____

List your reasons. ⟶ ______________________
____
____
____
____

To conclude ______________________

Repeat your point of view ⟶ ______________________
____

______________________ ⟵ Sign your name.

Yours ______________________

- **Re-write your letter as a discussion.**

Include other points of view. 

Teachers' note The children could use one of the arguments on pages 26 to 28 for this activity. It will be helpful if they have also completed pages 43 to 44. Revise the conventions of formal letter-writing and discuss how the style of a letter can be made appropriate for its audience. The children could write letters to a school newspaper or a local or national one to express their views about a topic.

Developing Literacy
Non-fiction Year 4
© A & C Black 2002

Write a discussion: 1

- **Use this page to help you plan a discussion.**

Topic to be discussed

- **Plan the discussion as a conversation.**
- **Write each character's point of view briefly in the speech bubble.**

Do not include reasons or evidence yet.

- **Give each character a name.**

- **Write each character's reasons or evidence.**

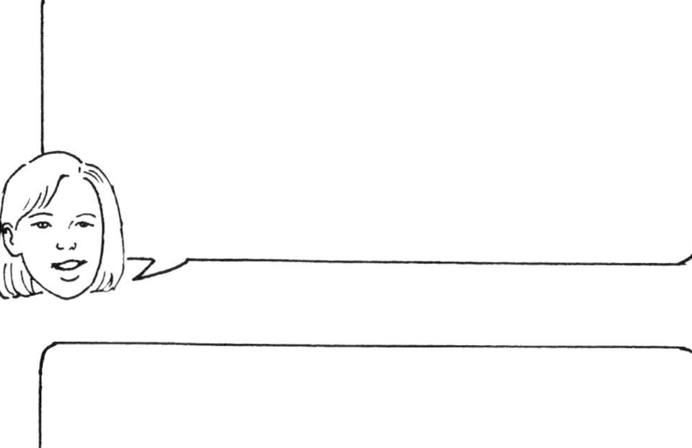

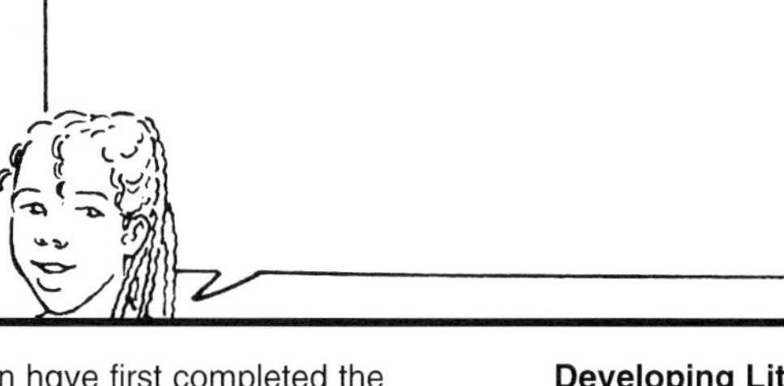

Teachers' note Use this with page 47. It will be helpful if the children have first completed the activity on page 29, which gives an example of a discussion. The discussion could be based on a topic of interest to the children. Note that in many discussions people begin by making assertions, but that they should then support the assertions with evidence or reasons. Continued on page 47.

Developing Literacy
Non-fiction Year 4
© A & C Black 2002

Write a discussion: 2

Your characters take part in a television discussion programme.

- **Write what they say.**

Write the characters' names in this column as for a playscript

Interviewer

On today's programme we have ______________, ____________, ______________ and ______________ to discuss ______________

____

____

____

____

____

____

____

____

____

____

____

____

____

Interviewer

In conclusion, ______________

____

____

Teachers' note Continued from page 46. It might be necessary to point out the difference between an argument and a discussion: an argument presents one point of view whereas a discussion presents several (although it might conclude by supporting one view).

**Developing Literacy
Non-fiction Year 4**
© A & C Black 2002

Plan an advertisement

- **Use this page to plan an advertisement.**

  Type of product _______________________

  Name of product

The impression I want people to have of the product

Adjectives to describe the product	**An alliterative slogan or a jingle**

Other words to create an impression

Verbs	**Adverbs**

Scientific words

How the product will make the customer feel special

Special offers

- **Using your notes, design your advertisement.**

It could be a poster, a magazine or newspaper advertisement, a leaflet, or a radio or television script.

Teachers' note The children should first read and listen to different types of advertisements, noticing the impressions they create and the ways in which the advertisers achieve this. It will be helpful if they have also completed the activities on pages 30 and 31.

Developing Literacy
Non-fiction Year 4
© A & C Black 2002